Seeing Revelation

A Guide for All Ages

Written and Illustrated by

Sarah Spann

For all of us who learn with pictures.

For my children: Jack and Lydia. You are loved more than you know.

For David: My best friend, love, and forever encourager. This would not have been possible without you.

For my mother – Renee Brundrett: The best teacher. The one who taught me to see the world like an artist

and to love God's Word.

In memory of my Daniel Bryant: Even If.

In seeing truth, we can know and worship God better.

Foreword

Revelation can be an intimidating book.

I have found that many people who have studied much of the Bible shy away from studying Revelation. But, did you know that it's the only book of the Bible with a special blessing attached? It says in Revelation 1:3 **" Blessed is he who reads and those who hear the words of the prophecy, and heed the things which are written in it; for the time is near."**

The time is near!

This book can be scary because much of it is about judgment. God is finally allowing justice to roll. He has been long-suffering and patient, and now we will see Him as the Great and Fair Judge.

But, another theme of Revelation is hope. For the believer, there is restoration, redemption, worship, and rest. There is no need to fear because there is One Who has been found Worthy – The Lion of Judah, the Root of David – Jesus Christ has overcome!

"And they sang a new song, saying, 'Worthy are You to take the book and to break its seals; for You were slain, and purchased for God with Your blood _men_ from every tribe and tongue and people and nation. You have made them _to be_ a kingdom and priests to our God; and they will reign upon the earth.'" (5:9-10)

Wow. Finally. The true King will take His place. And, believers will be restored to positions of reigning on the earth. The upside-downness of the world will be set right. The groaning will stop, and there will only be goodness.

I started this project to help myself and my kids "see Revelation" never intending it to become a book for others. In previous Bible studies, I would synthesize what I learned by drawing a one-page picture at the end of a study. Revelation demanded more drawings. It is so full of visuals! This book is formatted so that you read the chapter, reflect through questions, and then see it illustrated as it is written.

My hope is that we walk away from this knowing God better. I am praying that you respond in faith to Jesus' invitation to freely take His gift of life or worship Him with newfound gratitude for the life you have already received.

"The Spirit and the bride say, 'Come.' And let the one who hears say, 'Come.' And let the one who is thirsty come; let the one who wishes take the water of life without cost." Revelation 22:17

Love,

Sarah

Chapter 1

The Revelation of Jesus Christ, which God gave Him to show to His bond-servants, the things which must soon take place; and He sent and communicated it by His angel to His bond-servant John, who testified to the word of God and to the testimony of Jesus Christ, even to all that he saw. Blessed is he who reads and those who hear the words of the prophecy, and heed the things which are written in it; for the time is near.

John to the seven churches that are in Asia: Grace to you and peace, from Him who is and who was and who is to come, and from the seven Spirits who are before His throne, and from Jesus Christ, the faithful witness, the firstborn of the dead, and the ruler of the kings of the earth. To Him who loves us and released us from our sins by His blood— and He has made us to be a kingdom, priests to His God and Father—to Him be the glory and the dominion forever and ever. Amen. Behold, He is coming with the clouds, and every eye will see Him, even those who pierced Him; and all the tribes of the earth will mourn over Him. So it is to be. Amen.

"I am the Alpha and the Omega," says the Lord God, "who is and who was and who is to come, the Almighty."

I, John, your brother and fellow partaker in the tribulation and kingdom and perseverance which are in Jesus, was on the island called Patmos because of the word of God and the testimony of Jesus. I was in the Spirit on the Lord's day, and I heard behind me a loud voice like the sound of a trumpet, saying, "Write in a book what you see, and send it to the seven churches: to Ephesus and to Smyrna and to Pergamum and to Thyatira and to Sardis and to Philadelphia and to Laodicea."

Then I turned to see the voice that was speaking with me. And having turned I saw seven golden lampstands; and in the middle of the lampstands I saw one like a son of man, clothed in a robe reaching to the feet, and girded across His chest with a golden sash. His head and His hair were white like white wool, like snow; and His eyes were like a flame of fire. His feet were like burnished bronze, when it has been made to glow in a furnace, and His voice was like the sound of many waters. In His right hand He held seven stars, and out of His mouth came a sharp two-edged sword; and His face was like the sun shining in its strength.

When I saw Him, I fell at His feet like a dead man. And He placed His right hand on me, saying, "Do not be afraid; I am the first and the last, and the living One; and I was dead, and behold, I am alive forevermore, and I have the keys of death and of Hades. Therefore write the things which you have seen, and the things which are, and the things which will take place after these things. As for the mystery of the seven stars which you saw in My right hand, and the seven golden lampstands: the seven stars are the angels of the seven churches, and the seven lampstands are the seven churches.

Reflection Questions:

How do you apply prophecy to your life?

Are you ready for the Son of Man to return?

Chapter 2

"To the angel of the church in Ephesus write:

The One who holds the seven stars in His right hand, the One who walks among the seven golden lampstands, says this:

'I know your deeds and your toil and perseverance, and that you cannot tolerate evil men, and you put to the test those who call themselves apostles, and they are not, and you found them *to be* false; and you have perseverance and have endured for My name's sake, and have not grown weary. But I have *this* against you, that you have left your first love. Therefore remember from where you have fallen, and repent and do the deeds you did at first; or else I am coming to you and will remove your lampstand out of its place—unless you repent. Yet this you do have, that you hate the deeds of the Nicolaitans, which I also hate. He who has an ear, let him hear what the Spirit says to the churches. To him who overcomes, I will grant to eat of the tree of life which is in the Paradise of God.'

"And to the angel of the church in Smyrna write:

The first and the last, who was dead, and has come to life, says this:

'I know your tribulation and your poverty (but you are rich), and the blasphemy by those who say they are Jews and are not, but are a synagogue of Satan. Do not fear what you are about to suffer. Behold, the devil is about to cast some of you into prison, so that you will be tested, and you will have tribulation for ten days. Be faithful until death, and I will give you the crown of life. He who has an ear, let him hear what the Spirit says to the churches. He who overcomes will not be hurt by the second death.'

"And to the angel of the church in Pergamum write:

The One who has the sharp two-edged sword says this:

'I know where you dwell, where Satan's throne is; and you hold fast My name, and did not deny My faith even in the days of Antipas, My witness, My faithful one, who was killed among you, where Satan dwells. But I have a few things against you, because you have there some who hold the teaching of Balaam, who kept teaching Balak to put a stumbling block before the sons of Israel, to eat things sacrificed to idols and to commit *acts of* immorality. So you also have some who in the same way hold the teaching of the Nicolaitans. Therefore repent; or else I am coming to you quickly, and I will make war against them with the sword of My mouth. He who has an ear, let him hear what the Spirit says to the churches. To him who overcomes, to him I will give *some* of the hidden manna, and I will give him a white stone, and a new name written on the stone which no one knows but he who receives it.'

"And to the angel of the church in Thyatira write:

The Son of God, who has eyes like a flame of fire, and His feet are like burnished bronze, says this:

'I know your deeds, and your love and faith and service and perseverance, and that your deeds of late are greater than at first. But I have *this* against you, that you tolerate the woman Jezebel, who calls herself a prophetess, and she teaches and leads My bond-servants astray so that they commit *acts of* immorality and eat things sacrificed to idols. I gave her time to repent, and she does not want to repent of her immorality. Behold, I will throw her on a bed *of sickness*, and those who commit adultery with her into great tribulation, unless they repent of her deeds. And I will kill her children with pestilence, and all the churches will know that I am He who searches the minds and hearts; and I will give to each one of you according to your deeds. But I say to you, the rest who are in Thyatira, who do not hold this teaching, who have not known the deep things of Satan, as they call them—I place no other burden on you. Nevertheless what you have, hold fast until I come. He who overcomes, and he who keeps My deeds until the end, to him I will give authority over the nations; and he shall rule them with a rod of iron, as the vessels of the potter are broken to pieces, as I also have received *authority* from My Father; and I will give him the morning star. He who has an ear, let him hear what the Spirit says to the churches.'

Reflection Question:

What rewards can you identify for faithfulness?

Chapter 3

"To the angel of the church in Sardis write:

He who has the seven Spirits of God and the seven stars, says this: 'I know your deeds, that you have a name that you are alive, but you are dead. Wake up, and strengthen the things that remain, which were about to die; for I have not found your deeds completed in the sight of My God. So remember what you have received and heard; and keep *it*, and repent. Therefore if you do not wake up, I will come like a thief, and you will not know at what hour I will come to you. But you have a few people in Sardis who have not soiled their garments; and they will walk with Me in white, for they are worthy. He who overcomes will thus be clothed in white garments; and I will not erase his name from the book of life, and I will confess his name before My Father and before His angels. He who has an ear, let him hear what the Spirit says to the churches.'

"And to the angel of the church in Philadelphia write:

He who is holy, who is true, who has the key of David, who opens and no one will shut, and who shuts and no one opens, says this:

'I know your deeds. Behold, I have put before you an open door which no one can shut, because you have a little power, and have kept My word, and have not denied My name. Behold, I will cause *those* of the synagogue of Satan, who say that they are Jews and are not, but lie—I will make them come and bow down at your feet, and *make them* know that I have loved you. Because you have kept the word of My perseverance, I also will keep you from the hour of testing, that *hour* which is about to come upon the whole world, to test those who dwell on the earth. I am coming quickly; hold fast what you have, so that no one will take your crown. He who overcomes, I will make him a pillar in the temple of My God, and he will not go out from it anymore; and I will write on him the name of My God, and the name of the city of My God, the new Jerusalem, which comes down out of heaven from My God, and My new name. He who has an ear, let him hear what the Spirit says to the churches.'

"To the angel of the church in Laodicea write:

The Amen, the faithful and true Witness, the Beginning of the creation of God, says this:

'I know your deeds, that you are neither cold nor hot; I wish that you were cold or hot. So because you are lukewarm, and neither hot nor cold, I will spit you out of My mouth. Because you say, "I am rich, and have become wealthy, and have need of nothing," and you do not know that you are wretched and miserable and poor and blind and naked, I advise you to buy from Me gold refined by fire so that you may become rich, and white garments so that you may clothe yourself, and *that* the shame of your nakedness will not be revealed; and eye salve to anoint your eyes so that you may see. Those whom I love, I reprove and discipline; therefore be zealous and repent. Behold, I stand at the door and knock; if anyone hears My voice and opens the door, I will come in to him and will dine with him, and he with Me. He who overcomes, I will grant to him to sit down with Me on My throne, as I also overcame and sat down with My Father on His throne. He who has an ear, let him hear what the Spirit says to the churches.'"

Reflection Questions:

Your disobedient child is still your child.

That relationship is secure even if the rewards here and intimacy are at stake. If you are a believer already (a child of God- Galatians 3:26), do you need to confess anything that might be affecting your fellowship with Jesus?

If you are not a child of God, what is keeping you from believing?

Chapter 4

After these things I looked, and behold, a door *standing* open in heaven, and the first voice which I had heard, like *the sound* of a trumpet speaking with me, said, "Come up here, and I will show you what must take place after these things." Immediately I was in the Spirit; and behold, a throne was standing in heaven, and One sitting on the throne. And He who was sitting *was* like a jasper stone and a sardius in appearance; and *there was* a rainbow around the throne, like an emerald in appearance. Around the throne *were* twenty-four thrones; and upon the thrones *I saw* twenty-four elders sitting, clothed in white garments, and golden crowns on their heads.

Out from the throne come flashes of lightning and sounds and peals of thunder. And *there were* seven lamps of fire burning before the throne, which are the seven Spirits of God; and before the throne *there was something* like a sea of glass, like crystal; and in the center and around the throne, four living creatures full of eyes in front and behind. The first creature *was* like a lion, and the second creature like a calf, and the third creature had a face like that of a man, and the fourth creature *was* like a flying eagle. And the four living creatures, each one of them having six wings, are full of eyes around and within; and day and night they do not cease to say,

"Holy, holy, holy *is* the Lord God, the Almighty, who was and who is and who is to come."

And when the living creatures give glory and honor and thanks to Him who sits on the throne, to Him who lives forever and ever, the twenty-four elders will fall down before Him who sits on the throne, and will worship Him who lives forever and ever, and will cast their crowns before the throne, saying,

"Worthy are You, our Lord and our God, to receive glory and honor and power; for You created all things, and because of Your will they existed, and were created."

Reflection Questions:

Can you imagine worshipping God here? What are they praising God for? What can you praise Him for today?

19

Chapter 5

I saw in the right hand of Him who sat on the throne a book written inside and on the back, sealed up with seven seals. And I saw a strong angel proclaiming with a loud voice, "Who is worthy to open the book and to break its seals?" And no one in heaven or on the earth or under the earth was able to open the book or to look into it. Then I *began* to weep greatly because no one was found worthy to open the book or to look into it; and one of the elders said to me, "Stop weeping; behold, the Lion that is from the tribe of Judah, the Root of David, has overcome so as to open the book and its seven seals."

And I saw between the throne (with the four living creatures) and the elders a Lamb standing, as if slain, having seven horns and seven eyes, which are the seven Spirits of God, sent out into all the earth. And He came and took the book out of the right hand of Him who sat on the throne. When He had taken the book, the four living creatures and the twenty-four elders fell down before the Lamb, each one holding a harp and golden bowls full of incense, which are the prayers of the saints. And they sang a new song, saying,

"Worthy are You to take the book and to break its seals; for You were slain, and purchased for God with Your blood *men* from every tribe and tongue and people and nation. "You have made them *to be* a kingdom and priests to our God; and they will reign upon the earth."

Then I looked, and I heard the voice of many angels around the throne and the living creatures and the elders; and the number of them was myriads of myriads, and thousands of thousands, saying with a loud voice,

"Worthy is the Lamb that was slain to receive power and riches and wisdom and might and honor and glory and blessing."
And every created thing which is in heaven and on the earth and under the earth and on the sea, and all things in them, I heard saying,
"To Him who sits on the throne, and to the Lamb, *be* blessing and honor and glory and dominion forever and ever."

And the four living creatures kept saying, "Amen." And the elders fell down and worshiped.

Reflection Questions:

The Lamb has overcome! Who is the Lamb? And, why is He worthy of worship?

Chapter 6

Then I saw when the Lamb broke one of the seven seals, and I heard one of the four living creatures saying as with a voice of thunder, "Come." I looked, and behold, a white horse, and he who sat on it had a bow; and a crown was given to him, and he went out conquering and to conquer.

When He broke the second seal, I heard the second living creature saying, "Come." And another, a red horse, went out; and to him who sat on it, it was granted to take peace from the earth, and that *men* would slay one another; and a great sword was given to him.

When He broke the third seal, I heard the third living creature saying, "Come." I looked, and behold, a black horse; and he who sat on it had a pair of scales in his hand. And I heard *something* like a voice in the center of the four living creatures saying, "A quart of wheat for a denarius, and three quarts of barley for a denarius; and do not damage the oil and the wine."

When the Lamb broke the fourth seal, I heard the voice of the fourth living creature saying, "Come." I looked, and behold, an ashen horse; and he who sat on it had the name Death; and Hades was following with him. Authority was given to them over a fourth of the earth, to kill with sword and with famine and with pestilence and by the wild beasts of the earth.

When the Lamb broke the fifth seal, I saw underneath the altar the souls of those who had been slain because of the word of God, and because of the testimony which they had maintained; and they cried out with a loud voice, saying, "How long, O Lord, holy and true, will You refrain from judging and avenging our blood on those who dwell on the earth?" And there was given to each of them a white robe; and they were told that they should rest for a little while longer, until *the number of* their fellow servants and their brethren who were to be killed even as they had been, would be completed also.

I looked when He broke the sixth seal, and there was a great earthquake; and the sun became black as sackcloth *made* of hair, and the whole moon became like blood; and the stars of the sky fell to the earth, as a fig tree casts its unripe figs when shaken by a great wind. The sky was split apart like a scroll when it is rolled up, and every mountain and island were moved out of their places. Then the kings of the earth and the great men and the commanders and the rich and the strong and every slave and free man hid themselves in the caves and among the rocks of the mountains; and they said to the mountains and to the rocks, "Fall on us and hide us from the presence of Him who sits on the throne, and from the wrath of the Lamb; for the great day of their wrath has come, and who is able to stand?"

Reflection Questions:

This marks the beginning of the tribulation – Daniel's 70th week (see Daniel 9:27).

The Lord is described in this passage as "holy and true." God is always right therefore His justice is always right. How is that different from people? Can we be counted on to execute perfect justice?

28

4 come

5 how long ?

6

Chapter 7

After this I saw four angels standing at the four corners of the earth, holding back the four winds of the earth, so that no wind would blow on the earth or on the sea or on any tree. And I saw another angel ascending from the rising of the sun, having the seal of the living God; and he cried out with a loud voice to the four angels to whom it was granted to harm the earth and the sea, saying, "Do not harm the earth or the sea or the trees until we have sealed the bond-servants of our God on their foreheads."

And I heard the number of those who were sealed, one hundred and forty-four thousand sealed from every tribe of the sons of Israel:

from the tribe of Judah, twelve thousand *were* sealed, from the tribe of Reuben twelve thousand, from the tribe of Gad twelve thousand, from the tribe of Asher twelve thousand, from the tribe of Naphtali twelve thousand, from the tribe of Manasseh twelve thousand, from the tribe of Simeon twelve thousand, from the tribe of Levi twelve thousand, from the tribe of Issachar twelve thousand, from the tribe of Zebulun twelve thousand, from the tribe of Joseph twelve thousand, from the tribe of Benjamin, twelve thousand *were* sealed.

After these things I looked, and behold, a great multitude which no one could count, from every nation and *all* tribes and peoples and tongues, standing before the throne and before the Lamb, clothed in white robes, and palm branches *were* in their hands; and they cry out with a loud voice, saying,

"Salvation to our God who sits on the throne, and to the Lamb." And all the angels were standing around the throne and *around* the elders and the four living creatures; and they fell on their faces before the throne and worshiped God, saying,

"Amen, blessing and glory and wisdom and thanksgiving and honor and power and might, *be* to our God forever and ever. Amen."

Then one of the elders answered, saying to me, "These who are clothed in the white robes, who are they, and where have they come from?" I said to him, "My lord, you know." And he said to me, "These are the ones who come out of the great tribulation, and they have washed their robes and made them white in the blood of the Lamb. For this reason, they are before the throne of God; and they serve Him day and night in His temple; and He who sits on the throne will spread His tabernacle over them. They will hunger no longer, nor thirst anymore; nor will the sun beat down on them, nor any heat; for the Lamb in the center of the throne will be their shepherd, and will guide them to springs of the water of life; and God will wipe every tear from their eyes."

Reflection Question:

What are these worshippers praising God for?

Chapter 8

When the Lamb broke the seventh seal, there was silence in heaven for about half an hour. And I saw the seven angels who stand before God, and seven trumpets were given to them.

Another angel came and stood at the altar, holding a golden censer; and much incense was given to him, so that he might add it to the prayers of all the saints on the golden altar which was before the throne. And the smoke of the incense, with the prayers of the saints, went up before God out of the angel's hand. Then the angel took the censer and filled it with the fire of the altar, and threw it to the earth; and there followed peals of thunder and sounds and flashes of lightning and an earthquake.

And the seven angels who had the seven trumpets prepared themselves to sound them.

The first sounded, and there came hail and fire, mixed with blood, and they were thrown to the earth; and a third of the earth was burned up, and a third of the trees were burned up, and all the green grass was burned up.

The second angel sounded, and *something* like a great mountain burning with fire was thrown into the sea; and a third of the sea became blood, and a third of the creatures which were in the sea and had life, died; and a third of the ships were destroyed.

The third angel sounded, and a great star fell from heaven, burning like a torch, and it fell on a third of the rivers and on the springs of waters. The name of the star is called Wormwood; and a third of the waters became wormwood, and many men died from the waters, because they were made bitter.

The fourth angel sounded, and a third of the sun and a third of the moon and a third of the stars were struck, so that a third of them would be darkened and the day would not shine for a third of it, and the night in the same way.

Then I looked, and I heard an eagle flying in midheaven, saying with a loud voice, "Woe, woe, woe to those who dwell on the earth, because of the remaining blasts of the trumpet of the three angels who are about to sound!"

Reflection Questions:

Throughout Revelation, thunder, lightning, and earthquakes are repeated themes. Why do you think that is the case? Can you find them in the illustrations?

Chapter 9

Then the fifth angel sounded, and I saw a star from heaven which had fallen to the earth; and the key of the bottomless pit was given to him. He opened the bottomless pit, and smoke went up out of the pit, like the smoke of a great furnace; and the sun and the air were darkened by the smoke of the pit. Then out of the smoke came locusts upon the earth, and power was given them, as the scorpions of the earth have power. They were told not to hurt the grass of the earth, nor any green thing, nor any tree, but only the men who do not have the seal of God on their foreheads. And they were not permitted to kill anyone, but to torment for five months; and their torment was like the torment of a scorpion when it stings a man. And in those days men will seek death and will not find it; they will long to die, and death flees from them.

The appearance of the locusts was like horses prepared for battle; and on their heads appeared to be crowns like gold, and their faces were like the faces of men. They had hair like the hair of women, and their teeth were like *the teeth* of lions. They had breastplates like breastplates of iron; and the sound of their wings was like the sound of chariots, of many horses rushing to battle. They have tails like scorpions, and stings; and in their tails is their power to hurt men for five months. They have as king over them, the angel of the abyss; his name in Hebrew is Abaddon, and in the Greek he has the name Apollyon.

The first woe is past; behold, two woes are still coming after these things.

Then the sixth angel sounded, and I heard a voice from the four horns of the golden altar which is before God, one saying to the sixth angel who had the trumpet, "Release the four angels who are bound at the great river Euphrates." And the four angels, who had been prepared for the hour and day and month and year, were released, so that they would kill a third of mankind. The number of the armies of the horsemen was two hundred million; I heard the number of them. And this is how I saw in the vision the horses and those who sat on them: *the riders* had breastplates *the color* of fire and of hyacinth and of brimstone; and the heads of the horses are like the heads of lions; and out of their mouths proceed fire and smoke and brimstone. A third of mankind was killed by these three plagues, by the fire and the smoke and the brimstone which proceeded out of their mouths. For the power of the horses is in their mouths and in their tails; for their tails are like serpents and have heads, and with them they do harm.

The rest of mankind, who were not killed by these plagues, did not repent of the works of their hands, so as not to worship demons, and the idols of gold and of silver and of brass and of stone and of wood, which can neither see nor hear nor walk; and they did not repent of their murders nor of their sorceries nor of their immorality nor of their thefts.

Reflection Questions:

What do you notice about these trumpet judgments? Is there another place in the Bible we've seen something similar?

After all of this, why do you think people are still stubborn and unwilling to accept forgiveness?

Chapter 10

I saw another strong angel coming down out of heaven, clothed with a cloud; and the rainbow was upon his head, and his face was like the sun, and his feet like pillars of fire; and he had in his hand a little book which was open. He placed his right foot on the sea and his left on the land; and he cried out with a loud voice, as when a lion roars; and when he had cried out, the seven peals of thunder uttered their voices. When the seven peals of thunder had spoken, I was about to write; and I heard a voice from heaven saying, "Seal up the things which the seven peals of thunder have spoken and do not write them." Then the angel whom I saw standing on the sea and on the land lifted up his right hand to heaven, and swore by Him who lives forever and ever, who created heaven and the things in it, and the earth and the things in it, and the sea and the things in it, that there will be delay no longer, but in the days of the voice of the seventh angel, when he is about to sound, then the mystery of God is finished, as He preached to His servants the prophets.

Then the voice which I heard from heaven, *I heard* again speaking with me, and saying, "Go, take the book which is open in the hand of the angel who stands on the sea and on the land." So I went to the angel, telling him to give me the little book. And he said to me, "Take it and eat it; it will make your stomach bitter, but in your mouth it will be sweet as honey." I took the little book out of the angel's hand and ate it, and in my mouth it was sweet as honey; and when I had eaten it, my stomach was made bitter. And they said to me, "You must prophesy again concerning many peoples and nations and tongues and kings."

Chapter 11

Then there was given me a measuring rod like a staff; and someone said, "Get up and measure the temple of God and the altar, and those who worship in it. Leave out the court which is outside the temple and do not measure it, for it has been given to the nations; and they will tread under foot the holy city for forty-two months. And I will grant *authority* to my two witnesses, and they will prophesy for twelve hundred and sixty days, clothed in sackcloth." These are the two olive trees and the two lampstands that stand before the Lord of the earth. And if anyone wants to harm them, fire flows out of their mouth and devours their enemies; so if anyone wants to harm them, he must be killed in this way. These have the power to shut up the sky, so that rain will not fall during the days of their prophesying; and they have power over the waters to turn them into blood, and to strike the earth with every plague, as often as they desire.

When they have finished their testimony, the beast that comes up out of the abyss will make war with them, and overcome them and kill them. And their dead bodies *will lie* in the street of the great city which mystically is called Sodom and Egypt, where also their Lord was crucified. Those from the peoples and tribes and tongues and nations *will* look at their dead bodies for three and a half days, and will not permit their dead bodies to be laid in a tomb. And those who dwell on the earth *will* rejoice over them and celebrate; and they will send gifts to one another, because these two prophets tormented those who dwell on the earth.

But after the three and a half days, the breath of life from God came into them, and they stood on their feet; and great fear fell upon those who were watching them. And they heard a loud voice from heaven saying to them, "Come up here." Then they went up into heaven in the cloud, and their enemies watched them. And in that hour there was a great earthquake, and a tenth of the city fell; seven thousand people were killed in the earthquake, and the rest were terrified and gave glory to the God of heaven.

The second woe is past; behold, the third woe is coming quickly.

Then the seventh angel sounded; and there were loud voices in heaven, saying,

"The kingdom of the world has become *the kingdom* of our Lord and of His Christ; and He will reign forever and ever." And the twenty-four elders, who sit on their thrones before God, fell on their faces and worshiped God, saying,

"We give You thanks, O Lord God, the Almighty, who are and who were, because You have taken Your great power and have begun to reign. And the nations were enraged, and Your wrath came, and the time *came* for the dead to be judged, and *the time* to reward Your bond-servants the prophets and the saints and those who fear Your name, the small and the great, and to destroy those who destroy the earth."

And the temple of God which is in heaven was opened; and the ark of His covenant appeared in His temple, and there were flashes of lightning and sounds and peals of thunder and an earthquake and a great hailstorm.

Reflection Question:

John goes back here to fill in some gaps as to what has been happening during the tribulation in Jerusalem. Where do you see sorrow in these chapters, and where do you see hope?

Chapter 12

A great sign appeared in heaven: a woman clothed with the sun, and the moon under her feet, and on her head a crown of twelve stars; and she was with child; and she cried out, being in labor and in pain to give birth.

Then another sign appeared in heaven: and behold, a great red dragon having seven heads and ten horns, and on his heads *were* seven diadems. And his tail swept away a third of the stars of heaven and threw them to the earth. And the dragon stood before the woman who was about to give birth, so that when she gave birth he might devour her child.

And she gave birth to a son, a male *child*, who is to rule all the nations with a rod of iron; and her child was caught up to God and to His throne. Then the woman fled into the wilderness where she had a place prepared by God, so that there she would be nourished for one thousand two hundred and sixty days.

And there was war in heaven, Michael and his angels waging war with the dragon. The dragon and his angels waged war, and they were not strong enough, and there was no longer a place found for them in heaven. And the great dragon was thrown down, the serpent of old who is called the devil and Satan, who deceives the whole world; he was thrown down to the earth, and his angels were thrown down with him. Then I heard a loud voice in heaven, saying,

"Now the salvation, and the power, and the kingdom of our God and the authority of His Christ have come, for the accuser of our brethren has been thrown down, he who accuses them before our God day and night. And they overcame him because of the blood of the Lamb and because of the word of their testimony, and they did not love their life even when faced with death. For this reason, rejoice, O heavens and you who dwell in them. Woe to the earth and the sea, because the devil has come down to you, having great wrath, knowing that he has *only* a short time."

And when the dragon saw that he was thrown down to the earth, he persecuted the woman who gave birth to the male *child*. But the two wings of the great eagle were given to the woman, so that she could fly into the wilderness to her place, where she was nourished for a time and times and half a time, from the presence of the serpent. And the serpent poured water like a river out of his mouth after the woman, so that he might cause her to be swept away with the flood. But the earth helped the woman, and the earth opened its mouth and drank up the river which the dragon poured out of his mouth. So the dragon was enraged with the woman, and went off to make war with the rest of her children, who keep the commandments of God and hold to the testimony of Jesus.

*** special note. In Revelation, there are two Greek words used for "crown" and they are illustrated accordingly: 1) **stephanos** – a prize, usually a wreath or garland given to victors and 2) **diadema** – a kingly ornament, blue band marked with white which Persian kings used to bind on a turban.

In these diadema turbans, jewels were tucked in the folds to symbolize kingdoms that the kings had authority over. This context makes so much sense when we get to Revelation 19 and see the coming King of Kings with "many diadems".

Reflection Questions:

In this passage, we see Satan and various encounters of him through history and in the tribulation. The Bible calls him the "accuser of our brethren" in verse 10. But, Who are the Advocates for believers (1 John 2:1 and John 14:26)? What a team of lawyers!

How does that make you feel?

46

Chapter 13

And the dragon stood on the sand of the seashore.

Then I saw a beast coming up out of the sea, having ten horns and seven heads, and on his horns *were* ten diadems, and on his heads *were* blasphemous names. And the beast which I saw was like a leopard, and his feet were like *those* of a bear, and his mouth like the mouth of a lion. And the dragon gave him his power and his throne and great authority. *I saw* one of his heads as if it had been slain, and his fatal wound was healed. And the whole earth was amazed *and followed* after the beast; they worshiped the dragon because he gave his authority to the beast; and they worshiped the beast, saying, "Who is like the beast, and who is able to wage war with him?" There was given to him a mouth speaking arrogant words and blasphemies, and authority to act for forty-two months was given to him. And he opened his mouth in blasphemies against God, to blaspheme His name and His tabernacle, *that is*, those who dwell in heaven.

It was also given to him to make war with the saints and to overcome them, and authority over every tribe and people and tongue and nation was given to him. All who dwell on the earth will worship him, *everyone* whose name has not been written from the foundation of the world in the book of life of the Lamb who has been slain. If anyone has an ear, let him hear. If anyone *is destined* for captivity, to captivity he goes; if anyone kills with the sword, with the sword he must be killed. Here is the perseverance and the faith of the saints.

Then I saw another beast coming up out of the earth; and he had two horns like a lamb and he spoke as a dragon. He exercises all the authority of the first beast in his presence. And he makes the earth and those who dwell in it to worship the first beast, whose fatal wound was healed. He performs great signs, so that he even makes fire come down out of heaven to the earth in the presence of men. And he deceives those who dwell on the earth because of the signs which it was given him to perform in the presence of the beast, telling those who dwell on the earth to make an image to the beast who had the wound of the sword and has come to life. And it was given to him to give breath to the image of the beast, so that the image of the beast would even speak and cause as many as do not worship the image of the beast to be killed. And he causes all, the small and the great, and the rich and the poor, and the free men and the slaves, to be given a mark on their right hand or on their forehead, and *he provides* that no one will be able to buy or to sell, except the one who has the mark, *either* the name of the beast or the number of his name. Here is wisdom. Let him who has understanding calculate the number of the beast, for the number is that of a man; and his number is six hundred and sixty-six.

Reflection Questions:

The unholy, counterfeit trinity: The dragon (Satan), the beast (Antichrist), and the false prophet. The Devil cannot create, but he can imitate and replicate. Have you ever been deceived by Satan? How can we keep from being tricked?

Chapter 14

Then I looked, and behold, the Lamb *was* standing on Mount Zion, and with Him one hundred and forty-four thousand, having His name and the name of His Father written on their foreheads. And I heard a voice from heaven, like the sound of many waters and like the sound of loud thunder, and the voice which I heard *was* like *the sound* of harpists playing on their harps. And they sang a new song before the throne and before the four living creatures and the elders; and no one could learn the song except the one hundred and forty-four thousand who had been purchased from the earth. These are the ones who have not been defiled with women, for they have kept themselves chaste. These *are* the ones who follow the Lamb wherever He goes. These have been purchased from among men as first fruits to God and to the Lamb. And no lie was found in their mouth; they are blameless.

And I saw another angel flying in midheaven, having an eternal gospel to preach to those who live on the earth, and to every nation and tribe and tongue and people; and he said with a loud voice, "Fear God, and give Him glory, because the hour of His judgment has come; worship Him who made the heaven and the earth and sea and springs of waters."

And another angel, a second one, followed, saying, "Fallen, fallen is Babylon the great, she who has made all the nations drink of the wine of the passion of her immorality."

Then another angel, a third one, followed them, saying with a loud voice, "If anyone worships the beast and his image, and receives a mark on his forehead or on his hand, he also will drink of the wine of the wrath of God, which is mixed in full strength in the cup of His anger; and he will be tormented with fire and brimstone in the presence of the holy angels and in the presence of the Lamb. And the smoke of their torment goes up forever and ever; they have no rest day and night, those who worship the beast and his image, and whoever receives the mark of his name." Here is the perseverance of the saints who keep the commandments of God and their faith in Jesus.

And I heard a voice from heaven, saying, "Write, 'Blessed are the dead who die in the Lord from now on!'" "Yes," says the Spirit, "so that they may rest from their labors, for their deeds follow with them."

Then I looked, and behold, a white cloud, and sitting on the cloud *was* one like a son of man, having a golden crown on His head and a sharp sickle in His hand. And another angel came out of the temple, crying out with a loud voice to Him who sat on the cloud, "Put in your sickle and reap, for the hour to reap has come, because the harvest of the earth is ripe." Then He who sat on the cloud swung His sickle over the earth, and the earth was reaped.

And another angel came out of the temple which is in heaven, and he also had a sharp sickle. Then another angel, the one who has power over fire, came out from the altar; and he called with a loud voice to him who had the sharp sickle, saying, "Put in your sharp sickle and gather the clusters from the vine of the earth, because her grapes are ripe." So the angel swung his sickle to the earth and gathered *the clusters from* the vine of the earth, and threw them into the great wine press of the wrath of God. And the wine press was trodden outside the city, and blood came out from the wine press, up to the horses' bridles, for a distance of two hundred miles.

Reflection Questions:

Did you know that this is the only place in Scripture where you see an angel "flying" explicitly. In verse 6, an angel is flying and doing what? Preaching the gospel to all the people left! Wow. Do you know anyone who needs to hear the gospel today?

55

Chapter 15

Then I saw another sign in heaven, great and marvelous, seven angels who had seven plagues, *which are* the last, because in them the wrath of God is finished. And I saw something like a sea of glass mixed with fire, and those who had been victorious over the beast and his image and the number of his name, standing on the sea of glass, holding harps of God. And they sang the song of Moses, the bond-servant of God, and the song of the Lamb, saying,

"Great and marvelous are Your works,
O Lord God, the Almighty;
Righteous and true are Your ways,
King of the nations!
"Who will not fear, O Lord, and glorify Your name?
For You alone are holy;
For all the nations will come and worship before You,
For Your righteous acts have been revealed."

After these things I looked, and the temple of the tabernacle of testimony in heaven was opened, and the seven angels who had the seven plagues came out of the temple, clothed in linen, clean *and* bright, and girded around their chests with golden sashes. Then one of the four living creatures gave to the seven angels seven golden bowls full of the wrath of God, who lives forever and ever. And the temple was filled with smoke from the glory of God and from His power; and no one was able to enter the temple until the seven plagues of the seven angels were finished.

Chapter 16

Then I heard a loud voice from the temple, saying to the seven angels, "Go and pour out on the earth the seven bowls of the wrath of God."

So the first *angel* went and poured out his bowl on the earth; and it became a loathsome and malignant sore on the people who had the mark of the beast and who worshiped his image.

The second *angel* poured out his bowl into the sea, and it became blood like *that* of a dead man; and every living thing in the sea died.

Then the third *angel* poured out his bowl into the rivers and the springs of waters; and they became blood. And I heard the angel of the waters saying, "Righteous are You, who are and who were, O Holy One, because You judged these things; for they poured out the blood of saints and prophets, and You have given them blood to drink. They deserve it." And I heard the altar saying, "Yes, O Lord God, the Almighty, true and righteous are Your judgments."

The fourth *angel* poured out his bowl upon the sun, and it was given to it to scorch men with fire. Men were scorched with fierce heat; and they blasphemed the name of God who has the power over these plagues, and they did not repent so as to give Him glory.

Then the fifth *angel* poured out his bowl on the throne of the beast, and his kingdom became darkened; and they gnawed their tongues because of pain, and they blasphemed the God of heaven because of their pains and their sores; and they did not repent of their deeds.

The sixth *angel* poured out his bowl on the great river, the Euphrates; and its water was dried up, so that the way would be prepared for the kings from the east.

And I saw *coming* out of the mouth of the dragon and out of the mouth of the beast and out of the mouth of the false prophet, three unclean spirits like frogs; for they are spirits of demons, performing signs, which go out to the kings of the whole world, to gather them together for the war of the great day of God, the Almighty. ("Behold, I am coming like a thief. Blessed is the one who stays awake and keeps his clothes, so that he will not walk about naked and men will not see his shame.") And they gathered them together to the place which in Hebrew is called Har-Magedon.

Then the seventh *angel* poured out his bowl upon the air, and a loud voice came out of the temple from the throne, saying, "It is done." And there were flashes of lightning and sounds and peals of thunder; and there was a great earthquake, such as there had not been since man came to be upon the earth, so great an earthquake *was it, and* so mighty. The great city was split into three parts, and the cities of the nations fell. Babylon the great was remembered before God, to give her the cup of the wine of His fierce wrath. And every island fled away, and the mountains were not found. And huge hailstones, about one hundred pounds each, came down from heaven upon men; and men blasphemed God because of the plague of the hail, because its plague was extremely severe.

Reflection Questions:

If God did not remove all evil from earth before establishing His kingdom, we could question His justice. Could He really be good if He left sin unpunished and evil to have a foothold? No. Is it easier for you to accept God's love for you or His justice?

Great

① ② ③ ④

Chapter 17

Then one of the seven angels who had the seven bowls came and spoke with me, saying, "Come here, I will show you the judgment of the great harlot who sits on many waters, with whom the kings of the earth committed *acts of* immorality, and those who dwell on the earth were made drunk with the wine of her immorality." And he carried me away in the Spirit into a wilderness; and I saw a woman sitting on a scarlet beast, full of blasphemous names, having seven heads and ten horns. The woman was clothed in purple and scarlet, and adorned with gold and precious stones and pearls, having in her hand a gold cup full of abominations and of the unclean things of her immorality, and on her forehead a name *was* written, a mystery, "BABYLON THE GREAT, THE MOTHER OF HARLOTS AND OF THE ABOMINATIONS OF THE EARTH." And I saw the woman drunk with the blood of the saints, and with the blood of the witnesses of Jesus. When I saw her, I wondered greatly. And the angel said to me, "Why do you wonder? I will tell you the mystery of the woman and of the beast that carries her, which has the seven heads and the ten horns.

"The beast that you saw was, and is not, and is about to come up out of the abyss and go to destruction. And those who dwell on the earth, whose name has not been written in the book of life from the foundation of the world, will wonder when they see the beast, that he was and is not and will come. Here is the mind which has wisdom. The seven heads are seven mountains on which the woman sits, and they are seven kings; five have fallen, one is, the other has not yet come; and when he comes, he must remain a little while. The beast which was and is not, is himself also an eighth and is *one* of the seven, and he goes to destruction. The ten horns which you saw are ten kings who have not yet received a kingdom, but they receive authority as kings with the beast for one hour. These have one purpose, and they give their power and authority to the beast.

These will wage war against the Lamb, and the Lamb will overcome them, because He is Lord of lords and King of kings, and those who are with Him *are the* called and chosen and faithful."

And he said to me, "The waters which you saw where the harlot sits, are peoples and multitudes and nations and tongues. And the ten horns which you saw, and the beast, these will hate the harlot and will make her desolate and naked, and will eat her flesh and will burn her up with fire. For God has put it in their hearts to execute His purpose by having a common purpose, and by giving their kingdom to the beast, until the words of God will be fulfilled. The woman whom you saw is the great city, which reigns over the kings of the earth."

Reflection Questions:

This is a picture of religious "Babylon" (most people think this is a term used to describe the general evilness of the world system) about to fall. Throughout history, there have been world powers (Daniel 7). But, the kingdoms and kings of the earth rise up and then pass away. In the end, only one kingdom will stand. Which kingdom are you a citizen of and why?

Chapter 18

After these things I saw another angel coming down from heaven, having great authority, and the earth was illumined with his glory. And he cried out with a mighty voice, saying, "Fallen, fallen is Babylon the great! She has become a dwelling place of demons and a prison of every unclean spirit, and a prison of every unclean and hateful bird. For all the nations have drunk of the wine of the passion of her immorality, and the kings of the earth have committed *acts of* immorality with her, and the merchants of the earth have become rich by the wealth of her sensuality."

I heard another voice from heaven, saying, "Come out of her, my people, so that you will not participate in her sins and receive of her plagues; for her sins have piled up as high as heaven, and God has remembered her iniquities. Pay her back even as she has paid, and give back *to her* double according to her deeds; in the cup which she has mixed, mix twice as much for her. To the degree that she glorified herself and lived sensuously, to the same degree give her torment and mourning; for she says in her heart, 'I sit *as* a queen and I am not a widow, and will never see mourning.' For this reason in one day her plagues will come, pestilence and mourning and famine, and she will be burned up with fire; for the Lord God who judges her is strong.

"And the kings of the earth, who committed *acts of* immorality and lived sensuously with her, will weep and lament over her when they see the smoke of her burning, standing at a distance because of the fear of her torment, saying, 'Woe, woe, the great city, Babylon, the strong city! For in one hour your judgment has come.'

"And the merchants of the earth weep and mourn over her, because no one buys their cargoes any more— cargoes of gold and silver and precious stones and pearls and fine linen and purple and silk and scarlet, and every *kind of* citron wood and every article of ivory and every article *made* from very costly wood and bronze and iron and marble, and cinnamon and spice and incense and perfume and frankincense and wine and olive oil and fine flour and wheat and cattle and sheep, and *cargoes* of horses and chariots and slaves and human lives. The fruit you long for has gone from you, and all things that were luxurious and splendid have passed away from you and *men* will no longer find them. The merchants of these things, who became rich from her, will stand at a distance because of the fear of her torment, weeping and mourning, saying, 'Woe, woe, the great city, she who was clothed in fine linen and purple and scarlet, and adorned with gold and precious stones and pearls; for in one hour such great wealth has been laid waste!' And every shipmaster and every passenger and sailor, and as many as make their living by the sea, stood at a distance, and were crying out as they saw the smoke of her burning, saying, 'What *city* is like the great city?' And they threw dust on their heads and were crying out, weeping and mourning, saying, 'Woe, woe, the great city, in which all who had ships at sea became rich by her wealth, for in one hour she has been laid waste!' Rejoice over her, O heaven, and you saints and apostles and prophets, because God has pronounced judgment for you against her."

Then a strong angel took up a stone like a great millstone and threw it into the sea, saying, "So will Babylon, the great city, be thrown down with violence, and will not be found any longer. And the sound of harpists and musicians and flute-players and trumpeters will not be heard in you any longer; and no craftsman of any craft will be found in you any longer; and the sound of a mill will not be heard in you any longer; and the light of a lamp will not shine in you any longer; and the voice of the bridegroom and bride will not be heard in you any longer; for your merchants were the great men of the earth, because all the nations were deceived by your sorcery. And in her was found the blood of prophets and of saints and of all who have been slain on the earth."

Reflection Questions:

And, now economic Babylon is falling. Can you imagine watching the total destruction of a city and only being sad about your stuff? They disregard human life for wealth. Do you see examples of that happening today?

Chapter 19

19:1-10 – Marriage of the Lamb

After these things I heard something like a loud voice of a great multitude in heaven, saying,

"Hallelujah! Salvation and glory and power belong to our God; because His judgments are true and righteous; for He has judged the great harlot who was corrupting the earth with her immorality, and He has avenged the blood of His bond-servants on her." And a second time they said, "Hallelujah! Her smoke rises up forever and ever." And the twenty-four elders and the four living creatures fell down and worshiped God who sits on the throne saying, "Amen. Hallelujah!" And a voice came from the throne, saying,

"Give praise to our God, all you His bond-servants, you who fear Him, the small and the great." Then I heard *something* like the voice of a great multitude and like the sound of many waters and like the sound of mighty peals of thunder, saying,

"Hallelujah! For the Lord our God, the Almighty, reigns.

Let us rejoice and be glad and give the glory to Him, for the marriage of the Lamb has come and His bride has made herself ready." It was given to her to clothe herself in fine linen, bright *and* clean; for the fine linen is the righteous acts of the saints.

Then he said to me, "Write, 'Blessed are those who are invited to the marriage supper of the Lamb.'" And he said to me, "These are true words of God." Then I fell at his feet to worship him. But he said to me, "Do not do that; I am a fellow servant of yours and your brethren who hold the testimony of Jesus; worship God. For the testimony of Jesus is the spirit of prophecy."

19:17-21 – The Doom of the Beast and the False Prophet

Then I saw an angel standing in the sun, and he cried out with a loud voice, saying to all the birds which fly in midheaven, "Come, assemble for the great supper of God, so that you may eat the flesh of kings and the flesh of commanders and the flesh of mighty men and the flesh of horses and of those who sit on them and the flesh of all men, both free men and slaves, and small and great."

And I saw the beast and the kings of the earth and their armies assembled to make war against Him who sat on the horse and against His army.

And the beast was seized, and with him the false prophet who performed the signs in his presence, by which he deceived those who had received the mark of the beast and those who worshiped his image; these two were thrown alive into the lake of fire which burns with brimstone. And the rest were killed with the sword which came from the mouth of Him who sat on the horse, and all the birds were filled with their flesh.

Reflection Question:

What contrasting pictures! What do you notice about the differences in these scenes?

Chapter 19 Continued

19:11-16 – The Return of Christ!

And I saw heaven opened, and behold, a white horse, and He who sat on it *is* called Faithful and True, and in righteousness He judges and wages war.

His eyes *are* a flame of fire, and on His head *are* many diadems; and He has a name written *on Him* which no one knows except Himself.

He is clothed with a robe dipped in blood, and His name is called The Word of God.

And the armies which are in heaven, clothed in fine linen, white *and* clean, were following Him on white horses.

From His mouth comes a sharp sword, so that with it He may strike down the nations, and He will rule them with a rod of iron; and He treads the wine press of the fierce wrath of God, the Almighty. And on His robe and on His thigh He has a name written, "KING OF KINGS, AND LORD OF LORDS."

Reflection Questions:

This is such an amazing moment for Jesus and His redeemed. The True King leads His army into a battle that He has already won.

Have you ever been on a team that was guaranteed the victory? What does that feel like?

What do you observe about Christ in this passage?

This is the fulfillment of very important Old Testament prophecy. Read Psalm 2:9 and Isaiah 63:3 for more information.

***see note on page 45 about crowns.

75

Chapter 20

20:1:6

Then I saw an angel coming down from heaven, holding the key of the abyss and a great chain in his hand. And he laid hold of the dragon, the serpent of old, who is the devil and Satan, and bound him for a thousand years; and he threw him into the abyss, and shut *it* and sealed *it* over him, so that he would not deceive the nations any longer, until the thousand years were completed; after these things he must be released for a short time.

Then I saw thrones, and they sat on them, and judgment was given to them. And I *saw* the souls of those who had been beheaded because of their testimony of Jesus and because of the word of God, and those who had not worshiped the beast or his image, and had not received the mark on their forehead and on their hand; and they came to life and reigned with Christ for a thousand years. The rest of the dead did not come to life until the thousand years were completed. This is the first resurrection. Blessed and holy is the one who has a part in the first resurrection; over these the second death has no power, but they will be priests of God and of Christ and will reign with Him for a thousand years.

Millennial Kingdom

Isaiah 11:1-11
Then a shoot will spring from the stem of Jesse,
And a branch from his roots will bear fruit.
The Spirit of the Lord will rest on Him,
The spirit of wisdom and understanding,
The spirit of counsel and strength,
The spirit of knowledge and the fear of the Lord.
And He will delight in the fear of the Lord,
And He will not judge by what His eyes see,
Nor make a decision by what His ears hear;
But with righteousness He will judge the poor,
And decide with fairness for the afflicted of the earth;
And He will strike the earth with the rod of His mouth,
And with the breath of His lips He will slay the wicked.
Also righteousness will be the belt about His loins,
And faithfulness the belt about His waist.

And the wolf will dwell with the lamb,
And the leopard will lie down with the young goat,
And the calf and the young lion and the fatling together;
And a little boy will lead them.
Also the cow and the bear will graze,
Their young will lie down together,
And the lion will eat straw like the ox.
The nursing child will play by the hole of the cobra,
And the weaned child will put his hand on the viper's den.
They will not hurt or destroy in all My holy mountain,
For the earth will be full of the knowledge of the Lord
As the waters cover the sea.

Then in that day
The nations will resort to the root of Jesse,

Who will stand as a signal for the peoples;
And His resting place will be glorious.

Then it will happen on that day that the Lord
Will again recover the second time with His hand
The remnant of His people, who will remain…

Isaiah 65:20-25
No longer will there be in it an infant who lives but a few days,
Or an old man who does not live out his days;
For the youth will die at the age of one hundred
And the one who does not reach the age of one hundred
Will be thought accursed.
"They will build houses and inhabit them;
They will also plant vineyards and eat their fruit.
"They will not build and another inhabit,
They will not plant and another eat;
For as the lifetime of a tree, so will be the days of My people,
And My chosen ones will wear out the work of their hands.
"They will not labor in vain,
Or bear children for calamity;
For they are the offspring of those blessed by the Lord,
And their descendants with them.

It will also come to pass that before they call, I will answer; and while they are still speaking, I will hear. The wolf and the lamb will graze together, and the lion will eat straw like the ox; and dust will be the serpent's food. They will do no evil or harm in all My holy mountain," says the Lord.

Amos 9:13-15

"Behold, days are coming," declares the Lord,

"When the plowman will overtake the reaper

And the treader of grapes him who sows seed;

When the mountains will drip sweet wine

And all the hills will be dissolved.

"Also I will restore the captivity of My people Israel,

And they will rebuild the ruined cities and live *in them*;

They will also plant vineyards and drink their wine,

And make gardens and eat their fruit.

"I will also plant them on their land,

And they will not again be rooted out from their land

Which I have given them,"

Says the Lord your God.

Reflection Questions:

Satan is bound for 1000 years, and there is finally fulfillment of many promises made in the Old Testament. We see peace and justice on earth with Jesus' perfect rule. There's remarkable peace in the animal kingdom too. It's a time of abundance. But, it is also possible for people to procreate and die as some will not have glorified bodies.

Read through these passages. Can you find examples of peace with the animals?

Chapter 20 Continued

20:7-15

When the thousand years are completed, Satan will be released from his prison, and will come out to deceive the nations which are in the four corners of the earth, Gog and Magog, to gather them together for the war; the number of them is like the sand of the seashore. And they came up on the broad plain of the earth and surrounded the camp of the saints and the beloved city, and fire came down from heaven and devoured them. And the devil who deceived them was thrown into the lake of fire and brimstone, where the beast and the false prophet are also; and they will be tormented day and night forever and ever.

Then I saw a great white throne and Him who sat upon it, from whose presence earth and heaven fled away, and no place was found for them. And I saw the dead, the great and the small, standing before the throne, and books were opened; and another book was opened, which is *the book* of life; and the dead were judged from the things which were written in the books, according to their deeds. And the sea gave up the dead which were in it, and death and Hades gave up the dead which were in them; and they were judged, every one *of them* according to their deeds. Then death and Hades were thrown into the lake of fire. This is the second death, the lake of fire. And if anyone's name was not found written in the book of life, he was thrown into the lake of fire.

Reflection Questions:

This section is known as the "Great White Throne" Judgment, and it is only for unbelievers – those whose names are not written in the Lamb's book of Life who will consequently be judged by their deeds and found guilty.

The Judgment Seat of Christ (Bema seat) is a judgment for believers that is referenced many times in the New Testament (1 Corinthians 3; 2 Corinthians 5:10). And, it is a judgment for reward - not whether a person goes to heaven or hell. That is not pictured here.

Which judgment will you be attending? Why?

If you are a believer in Jesus, your name is in His book and you are forever sealed in His family.

Chapter 21

Then I saw a new heaven and a new earth; for the first heaven and the first earth passed away, and there is no longer *any* sea. And I saw the holy city, new Jerusalem, coming down out of heaven from God, made ready as a bride adorned for her husband. And I heard a loud voice from the throne, saying, "Behold, the tabernacle of God is among men, and He will dwell among them, and they shall be His people, and God Himself will be among them, and He will wipe away every tear from their eyes; and there will no longer be *any* death; there will no longer be *any* mourning, or crying, or pain; the first things have passed away."

And He who sits on the throne said, "Behold, I am making all things new." And He said, "Write, for these words are faithful and true." Then He said to me, "It is done. I am the Alpha and the Omega, the beginning and the end. I will give to the one who thirsts from the spring of the water of life without cost. He who overcomes will inherit these things, and I will be his God and he will be My son. But for the cowardly and unbelieving and abominable and murderers and immoral persons and sorcerers and idolaters and all liars, their part *will be* in the lake that burns with fire and brimstone, which is the second death."

Then one of the seven angels who had the seven bowls full of the seven last plagues came and spoke with me, saying, "Come here, I will show you the bride, the wife of the Lamb."

And he carried me away in the Spirit to a great and high mountain, and showed me the holy city, Jerusalem, coming down out of heaven from God, having the glory of God. Her brilliance was like a very costly stone, as a stone of crystal-clear jasper. It had a great and high wall, with twelve gates, and at the gates twelve angels; and names *were* written on them, which are *the names* of the twelve tribes of the sons of Israel. *There were* three gates on the east and three gates on the north and three gates on the south and three gates on the west. And the wall of the city had twelve foundation stones, and on them *were* the twelve names of the twelve apostles of the Lamb.

The one who spoke with me had a gold measuring rod to measure the city, and its gates and its wall. The city is laid out as a square, and its length is as great as the width; and he measured the city with the rod, fifteen hundred miles; its length and width and height are equal. And he measured its wall, seventy-two yards, *according to* human measurements, which are *also* angelic *measurements*. The material of the wall was jasper; and the city was pure gold, like clear glass. The foundation stones of the city wall were adorned with every kind of precious stone. The first foundation stone was jasper; the second, sapphire; the third, chalcedony; the fourth, emerald; the fifth, sardonyx; the sixth, sardius; the seventh, chrysolite; the eighth, beryl; the ninth, topaz; the tenth, chrysoprase; the eleventh, jacinth; the twelfth, amethyst. And the twelve gates were twelve pearls; each one of the gates was a single pearl. And the street of the city was pure gold, like transparent glass.

I saw no temple in it, for the Lord God the Almighty and the Lamb are its temple. And the city has no need of the sun or of the moon to shine on it, for the glory of God has illumined it, and its lamp *is* the Lamb. The nations will walk by its light, and the kings of the earth will bring their glory into it. In the daytime (for there will be no night there) its gates will never be closed; and they will bring the glory and the honor of the nations into it; and nothing unclean, and no one who practices abomination and lying, shall ever come into it, but only those whose names are written in the Lamb's book of life.

Reflection Questions:

It's finally here – the new heaven and the new earth! The tabernacle of God finally among men! Can you imagine Jesus wiping away your tears and then living in a place where there was never any sadness or pain? And, it is free to live here. The gospel says that it cost Jesus much – His death on a cross, but He offers you forgiveness FREELY – truly without cost (John 3:16).

Let that sink into your heart.

Have you put your faith in Jesus alone for the forgiveness of your sins? Or, are you trying to earn acceptance into His kingdom another way? The radical message of the gospel of grace is that you do NOT deserve it, but God rescues you anyway. He's the only One Who could.

Chapter 22

Then he showed me a river of the water of life, clear as crystal, coming from the throne of God and of the Lamb, in the middle of its street. On either side of the river was the tree of life, bearing twelve *kinds of* fruit, yielding its fruit every month; and the leaves of the tree were for the healing of the nations. There will no longer be any curse; and the throne of God and of the Lamb will be in it, and His bond-servants will serve Him; they will see His face, and His name *will be* on their foreheads. And there will no longer be *any* night; and they will not have need of the light of a lamp nor the light of the sun, because the Lord God will illumine them; and they will reign forever and ever.

And he said to me, "These words are faithful and true"; and the Lord, the God of the spirits of the prophets, sent His angel to show to His bond-servants the things which must soon take place.

"And behold, I am coming quickly. Blessed is he who heeds the words of the prophecy of this book."

I, John, am the one who heard and saw these things. And when I heard and saw, I fell down to worship at the feet of the angel who showed me these things. But he *said to me, "Do not do that. I am a fellow servant of yours and of your brethren the prophets and of those who heed the words of this book. Worship God."

And he said to me, "Do not seal up the words of the prophecy of this book, for the time is near. Let the one who does wrong, still do wrong; and the one who is filthy, still be filthy; and let the one who is righteous, still practice righteousness; and the one who is holy, still keep himself holy."

"Behold, I am coming quickly, and My reward *is* with Me, to render to every man according to what he has done. I am the Alpha and the Omega, the first and the last, the beginning and the end."

Blessed are those who wash their robes, so that they may have the right to the tree of life, and may enter by the gates into the city. Outside are the dogs and the sorcerers and the immoral persons and the murderers and the idolaters, and everyone who loves and practices lying.

"I, Jesus, have sent My angel to testify to you these things for the churches. I am the root and the descendant of David, the bright morning star."

The Spirit and the bride say, "Come." And let the one who hears say, "Come." And let the one who is thirsty come; let the one who wishes take the water of life without cost.

I testify to everyone who hears the words of the prophecy of this book: if anyone adds to them, God will add to him the plagues which are written in this book; and if anyone takes away from the words of the book of this prophecy, God will take away his part from the tree of life and from the holy city, which are written in this book.

He who testifies to these things says, "Yes, I am coming quickly." Amen. Come, Lord Jesus.

The grace of the Lord Jesus be with all. Amen.

Reflection Questions:

Jesus is coming quickly! Are you ready? Are the people you know and love ready?

Final Thoughts

We did it! We went on a journey through Revelation together. God's final letter is challenging but also invitational.

There is a distinct line drawn. People were made in the image of God and will eventually live forever. Did you realize that immortality is part of your future? There is no such thing as total annihilation for human beings. So, the question is: "In which kingdom will you live in for eternity?" There are only 2 options: with God or eternally separated from God.

If you have never heard the gospel, it is my absolute privilege to share this news with you:

1) You were created by God. He loves you and has a wonderful plan for you.
   "For You formed my inward parts; You wove me in my mother's womb. I will give thanks to You, for I am fearfully and wonderfully made..." Psalm 139:13,14a

2) But, there's bad news. You are a sinner. "Sin" means to miss the mark. The Bible says that everyone has sin.
   "for all have sinned and fall short of the glory of God" Romans 3:23

3) More bad news. The penalty for sin is death – death means eternal separation from God. Sin must be judged.
   "For the wages of sin is death, but the free gift of God is eternal life in Christ Jesus our Lord." Romans 6:23

4) The greatest news ever! Jesus Christ died for you and then rose from the dead! He took your place and paid the price for your sin in full so that you could be 100% forgiven forever.
   "But God demonstrates His own love toward us, in that while we were yet sinners, Christ died for us." Romans 5:8

5) This salvation, forgiveness, and place in God's kingdom is offered to you freely. You can be saved through FAITH alone in Jesus Christ. Believe. You cannot earn salvation. You don't deserve it. It is a gift to receive.
   "For by grace you have been saved through faith; and that not of yourselves, *it is* the gift of God; not as a result of works, so that no one may boast." Ephesians 2:8,9
   "For God so loved the world, that He gave His only begotten Son, that whoever believes in Him shall not perish, but have eternal life." John 3:16

Have you believed? You can trust Jesus today.

www.ingramcontent.com/pod-product-compliance
Lightning Source LLC
Chambersburg PA
CBHW040816120626

46551CB00004B/570